The Unreasonable Slug

Also by Matt Cook:

*In the Small of My Backyard*
*Eavesdrop Soup*

# The Unreasonable Slug

Matt Cook

Manic D Press
San Francisco

Cover photo © Elroy Serrao
Printed in the USA


*Library of Congress Cataloging-in-Publication Data*

Cook, Matt, 1969-
  The unreasonable slug / Matt Cook.
    p. cm.
  ISBN 978-1-933149-15-8 (trade pbk.)
  1. Milwaukee (Wis.)–Poetry. I. Title.
PS3603.O574U57 2007
811'.6–dc22
                              2007012451

*for John McEwan,*
*who said wise things quietly;*
*I took them, said them louder,*
*And got all the credit.*

The imagination is innately a biological power seeking to overcome impossible conditions.

— *Saul Bellow*

# Contents

III.

IV.

I.

Rest Assured

I remember them using that insult against me before,
But I remember it hurting more last time.
I have memories that I'm not using very often
That I would be happy to give to someone who needed memories.
My petty concerns never really got the credit they deserved.
My petty concerns probably suffered from poor packaging.
My reasonable doubts seemed perfectly reasonable at the time,
But later on, when it was really important, they seemed unreasonable.
I don't frankly remember if there was a moon last night.
Sometimes you can tell halfway through a story
That you're making a mistake by telling that story.
Rest assured, this feeling of invincibility will pass.

The Modernist Bowling Alley

The forgotten soul who first separated egg whites.
The homeless man wearing the *Superman* t-shirt.
Their intentions were clearly understood,
Except when they were unintentional and misunderstood.
The gypsy moth is no longer destroying the prized sweaters
With anywhere near his previous curve of frequency.
Shoddy construction is now the more critical threat.
The modernist bowling alley will have the futuristic waiting area
Where you can go and wait patiently for the future.
You will see a clock on the wall that doesn't really look like a clock.
You will distinctly remember having forgotten that before.

The City Feels Different

The city feels different when your best friend is out of town.
More people are driving their cars with their elbows out the window.
People are expressing social alienation through ill-fitting trousers.
The young man is pouring his depleted heart into a mobile telephone.
Every neighborhood is either too nice or not nice enough.
You feel more comfortable in the neighborhoods that are not nice enough.
It's partly cloudy and partly windy and partly cold.
When you ask someone for directions,
You follow those directions until you can no longer remember them,
And then you ask a new person.

The Hands of Boiled Wieners

When we hear the croaking of the bullfrogs
We never assume the croaking to be disingenuous.
We never propound on the notion of insincere bullfrogs.
When we tie our shoes during a dream,
The dream can overcomplicate the situation.
Disappointment can overwhelm you simply by opening a suitcase.
Given time, everyone will suffer
Personal abasement at the hands of boiled wieners.
The boundaries of sense were accidentally uncovered
Through deliberate experiments with nonsense:
The elder statesman and the satiated welder in the station wagon,
The origin of the porridge in the corridor,
The dream and the poem and the hangover have all been in this situation.

Back Together Again

Your childhood memories are the only childhood memories you have.
Your father is usually the first man you see light a fuse and run away.
You have a childhood memory of an instant
Replay of a car exploding on a racetrack.
Your grandfather predicted that rye bread
Would outlast the internal combustion engine.
Why are we so impressed when someone can take
Something apart and put it back together again?

## Asking Someone

We probably need to set aside
More time in our relationship
For arguments about factory farming.
Cynicism may be unhealthy
But that does not make it incorrect.
The alternatives to cynicism will not bring you happiness.
The snot-nosed man entering
The building through the side door
Will not bring you happiness.
The sound of nothing in the hallway.
Ignorance may be the last frontier.
I didn't *know* that ignorance of the law was no excuse.
Some of the best people don't know the way to San Jose.
We shouldn't be so judgmental
When someone doesn't know the way to San Jose.
Sometimes the redundant man is only attempting to be musical.
Redundancy *is* musical.
The nickel that was so old it was worth more than a nickel.
The coin collector who was broke because he spent all his money on coins.
The penniless coin collector. He should have collected pennies.
I wonder what it's like to command no respect.
I probably could find out
By *asking* someone who commands no respect.

A Convincing Swan

Forcing oneself to write imaginative literature
Is something like forcing oneself to draw a convincing swan.
That is, a swan that can be taken seriously as a swan,
A lagoon that does not dishonor a lagoon.
Grabbing a bull by the horns is probably
One of the stupidest things a man can do.
Developing a taste for water chestnuts usually involves
Waiting around until you like the taste of water chestnuts.
When you are fortunate, though, you will not need to wait around.
When you are fortunate, *someone else* will force you
To draw a convincing swan.

Winslow

He wrote poems that made it more fun to sit in a chair.
He would take extension bridges, so to speak, and then he would
Force them, against their will, to span the Delaware River.
He once left his hat outside in the rain,
And then it shrunk until it fit his little brother.

If only people understood
How impressive his stomach cramps were.
Why did the burden always fall on him
To explain his stomach cramps to people?

He made his own pickles down in his basement.
He liked making his own pickles down in his basement,
Because it took longer that way and it was more expensive
And the pickles tasted wrong.
We belittled his achievements and we held him up to ridicule.
We bought pickles made in large facilities, and we laughed in his face.

When will the revolting conditions be randomly imposed?
The redistribution of wealth, as a general principle,
Never really gripped people the way we wanted it to.
Perhaps misery is more malleable.
Perhaps misery could find equitable distribution.
Squalid conditions could be arranged alphabetically, boy girl, boy girl.
People standing around in the sun doing things over and over again.

I knew a man who was mad at the world,
And then he sat in his car all night talking to himself,
And that really showed the world.
His unfounded anger was dispelled by an explanation that made no sense.
You need an explanation that makes no sense to dispel unfounded anger.
He thought his teacups were bugged by the federal authorities.
It's self-important to think the government is interested in you.

The average man will approach you with unhelpful suggestions.
Mediocrity is cruel and unusual; incompetence does not discriminate.
Incompetence can be beautiful when it's wearing a mulberry pullover.

## The Poet's Handshake

The sidewalk will anticipate the pedestrian.
How *presumptuous* of the sidewalk to do that.
How presumptuous of the loading dock to suggest what it suggests.
What if they built a loading dock and nobody came and loaded anything?

The gumball machine will operate in its own cruel way.
The gumball machine will reward the child with access to capital.
The creaking door will sound more like the crying baby
Than the crying baby will sound like the creaking door.
The beginning poet will chronicle the debris on his countertop.
If the poet's handshake is too firm he loses credibility.

Do you remember that man who became famous when he attached
Lie detectors to plants and wrote a book about it?
He sincerely believed that plants could fall in love
And petition the government for a redress of grievances.

## So Anti War

He was so anti-war that even the anti-war people couldn't stand him.
He was so anti-war that critics of the administration
Would cross the street to avoid him.
His opposition to the war was more sophisticated,
And frankly superior to your opposition to the war.
He could prove that he was more anti-war than you were.
His parents were more anti-war than your parents.
His *apartment* was more anti-war than your apartment.
He had read studies that you hadn't read
That proved that what you read was wrong.
He was *too* anti-war for the anti-war people.
He was so anti-war that the anti-war people
Stopped inviting him to their barbecues.
He was absolutely right about everything all the time—
Even when it had nothing to do with the war.
His position on energy-efficient storm windows
Was superior to your position on energy-efficient storm windows.
He was so self-righteous
That cocaine addicts thought he was a born-again Christian.
He said that trying not to look at an Amish person
Was actually more insensitive than looking at an Amish person.
He was certain that barbed concertina wire
Was originally inspired by thorny shrubs.
If something was wrong with your car,
He was right about what was wrong with your car.
His knowledge of automotive voltage regulators was uncanny

And seemed at odds with his general Bohemianism.

He had evidence that tropical ants had fought unjust wars

Against rival colonies driven by incompetent leadership.

He was so anti-war that he wouldn't let anybody else talk about the war.

But he didn't like talking about the war alone—

He wanted other people around that he could *interrupt* about the war.

He wanted to tell you how to raise your anti-war children.

The children, he said, should be homeschooled, restricted to basements,

And made to wear helmets of reinforced plastic.

He was so anti-war that even the anti-war people did not like him.

But I liked him.

II.

Everybody and their Mother


He was sober as a judge, but he wasn't a judge,

He was a Disney worker in a furry suit, or he felt like one.

He had too many earrings before it was stupid to have too many earrings.

He was unoriginal when unoriginal wasn't cool.

He was not afraid of death or prison or icy roads,

But he was afraid of his mother's boyfriend's coffee grinder.

He was willing to die for his country, but he was not

Willing to be confined to a wheelchair for his country.

One needs to be modest about one's modesty.

The drunk driver.

The drunk bus driver.

The drunk school bus driver.

The pregnant drunk school bus driver.

The compulsive liars should be listed in the telephone directory.

You should be able to buy insurance

Against becoming a parody of yourself.

Hardly responding to *Yes* and *No* questions.

Drawing the indiscriminate birds in the sky,

The rats in the pipes below Harvard,

The underwater spiders, their dwellings of airtight silk.

This poem is a dog's breakfast, but why begrudge a dog his breakfast?

Everybody and their mother

Lost their lunch over the Bohemian coin laundry goddess.

Every leaf is not a poem; that needs to be reconsidered.

For my purposes, snowflakes are all pretty much the same.

More Ordinary

People will continue to become excited
When the days grow longer in the springtime—
It's the prospect of watching
Television during extended daylight.
Some ordinary Americans are
More ordinary than other ordinary Americans.
You're either too lonely or not lonely enough.
Finding Jesus Christ has become easier than finding your car keys.
It's not the singer, it's the song; it's not the cooper, it's the barrel.
The elitist disparagement of puffy
Armchairs favored by the laboring classes.
It's too easy to bear false witness against the automobile driver
With his processed food and his greasy steering wheel.
When will the plumage of the ducks achieve standardization?
When will the proper authorities establish independent criteria?

Bogged Down


Not doing anything will remind you of other times you did nothing.
The human condition can really cut into your days sometimes.
The stars in the sky will have surprisingly few stories to tell.
Sometimes the wrong things will break,
Like the windbreaker with the broken zipper.
Walking uphill with no money in your pocket and your zipper's broken.
Your sleeves are too short and it changes your life in meaningful ways.
The assorted dumbasses are standing around the courtyard.
The cockroaches are eating the garbage under the moonlight.
Your sleeves are too short and your zipper is broken.
The cockroaches have defined garbage differently than you have.
You and the cockroaches are always getting bogged down in definitions.

The White Guy

The white guy wearing the white guy shirt.
Asking you a lot of white guy questions.
Standing in the white guy line.
Filling out a lot of white guy forms.
Reaching down to pick up some white guy thing on the floor.
Using some white guy pretext to get your attention.
Going around and around in white guy circles.
Falling out of the white guy trees in November.

The Woman Next Door

The woman next door
Was in the process of getting evicted.
The landlord had shut her power off.
She had all this meat in her freezer, she said.
She was really worried about the meat in her freezer.
She wondered if I had a long extension cord
That we could run between our houses
To keep her freezer running
Until she moved into a new apartment.
I plugged an extension cord into a kitchen outlet
And ran the cord out my kitchen window
And in through her kitchen window.
The cord was there like that for days and days
And I felt good about the whole thing.
It felt good to be keeping somebody else's meat cold.
And then one day she was gone.
Her car was gone, she was gone, everything.
And my extension cord was gone.
She stole my freaking extension cord—
Weirdo ungrateful extension cord thief.

Serenity

He understood that the morning glories
Were only glorious in the morning.
But he was an alcoholic,
And he slept until the early afternoon.
So that by the time he woke up,
The morning glories were no longer glorious.

Either the morning glories were going to have to change,
Or he was going to have to change.

Probably

We need to discuss these ideas
Before we can finish discussing these ideas.
If we thought about these ideas some more,
We could probably make them better.
They probably could have invented
The Frisbee *sooner* if they had only tried *harder.*
But the Frisbee probably would have seemed
Inappropriate during the Great Depression.

The outcome of a disagreement can sometimes be
Influenced by hurling crockery.
One man's coat rack is another man's shower rod.
Matrimony can involve disagreements
Concerning landscaping boulders.
When will the slotted screws and the
Phillips screws set aside their differences?
How long will it take before the identical twins
Feel comfortable playing dominoes together?

Recyclables


Saw a Buddhist temple in Illinois,
Operating out of a defunct fish and chips franchise building,
Where, one could still see, undismayed, the nautical rope motif
Leftover from the defunct fish and chips franchise building.
The worshippers, apparently, were fine with the nautical rope motif.
The heroic *pigweed* was growing through a crack in the foundation.
The broken bottles were in the gutter—
The unbroken bottles were in the gutter.
The hillbillies on LSD
Were controlling the roller coaster in the parking lot.

What is weird will become less weird until it isn't weird anymore,
Which will be weird, for a while, but then that will pass,
And then the whole thing will never be weird again.
Standing downwind from commingled recyclables.
The Frederic Remington drawing of a cowboy.
The Frederic Remington drawing of an Indian.

Mormon Underwear


I Googled "Mormon underwear" because someone told me to do that.
I found out that Mormon underwear protects you from the world.
That's what it said on the Internet.
It said that Mormon underwear protects you from the world.
It also said that a Mormon can tell whether or not
You're wearing Mormon underwear.
It didn't say how exactly a Mormon could tell this.
But I'm guessing a Mormon can probably surmise this through
A nuanced understanding of the rumples in one's trousers.
And because of this, because a Mormon can tell if you're wearing,
Shrewd trial lawyers in Utah will usually own a pair of Mormon underwear
To give them an advantage in the courtroom.
That's what it said on the Internet.
It also probably protects them from the world.

Better Than Something

He brought hope to millions, but it was false hope,
So actually he had not brought hope to millions.
But he hadn't exactly brought nothing, either—
He brought false hope, which was about like nothing,
But it was more involved than nothing, it was better than nothing,
It was what people wanted back before they wanted nothing.
People had been waiting around all morning for false hope.
It was like waiting around all morning for nothing,
But it was better than waiting around all morning for nothing.
It was almost like having something for nothing,
But it was like having to wait around all morning for it.

## Something in Common

He would get angry if your hands were cold
And you ran them under hot water.
He had some reason why that was bad.
The situation came up more often than you thought.
You maintain your superstitions or they fall into disbelief.
He had an unspecified number of ballpoint pens in his shoulder bag.
His enemies were just satisfied that he was failing.
The rain was coming in through his ceiling
Because his ceiling wasn't really a ceiling
It was more like a hole in the ceiling.
An unspecified number of ballpoint pens in his shoulder bag.
We had nothing in common except that
Our grandfathers lived in Pennsylvania,
Even though my grandfather didn't live in Pennsylvania.
I only pretended that my grandfather lived in Pennsylvania
In order to have something in common with this guy.

The Paper Bag

There are tiny little numbers that make no sense
On the bottoms of most paper bags in America.
It's like finding part of an insect on a windowsill.
Like finding someone else's hair inside a library book.
A slim volume of not terrible Turkish poetry.
The paper bag standing upright on the kitchen floor.
The paper bag affording opportunity for the domestic cat.
The cat will make sense out of the paper bag—
Sense that will not necessarily make sense to you.
The cat may or may not appreciate the reorganized utility closet.
The cat may or may not appreciate
The paper bag breaking six ways from Sunday.

To Count the Cars or Whatever

The opera company will not post advertisements on telephone poles,
Despite the many opera lovers who walk past telephone poles.
The public library will get all uptight
When you've had their materials for too long.
The circulation aid will have a hammer and sickle tattooed on his neck.
You will pause rather than encourage him further.

The customer service representative will seem eager to disappoint you.
You're aware that chicken feed is famously inexpensive,
But you understand that chicken feed doesn't exist in a vacuum.

That rubber cord they stretch across
The road to count the cars or whatever.
The reasonable expectation of the cars driving down the road.

They will give your best friend a ticket for parking too much.
When will they give out gift certificates to the police station?
When will they criminalize the comfortable chairs?

Important men no longer have globes in their offices.
With proper diet and exercise you can
Outlive the authority figures in your life.

Some Days

Some days you're just not in the mood for a spirited debate.
The authorities will say that the blossom-end rot was caused by either
Too much water, not enough water, or just the right amount of water.
One's position regarding the future is always constructed
To make one appear respectable in the present.
The wolf spider in the mailbox has no idea that it's Thursday.
What that pigeon needs is a good ten cent windowsill.
The wise maxims should be available in your grocer's freezer.
The wolf spider in the mailbox has no idea that it's Thursday.
It's anybody's guess how the wolf spider breaks up his week.
He probably breaks it up with achievements.

The Mediocre Lunch

The mediocre lunch can be an inspiration.
When the inspiration of the mediocre lunch fades,
Then's when you've got problems.
You look out the window,
You feel sorry for the bike left out in the snow.
But the alternatives to the bike left out in the snow are unsettling,
Beginning with, the bike *not* left out in the snow.
You can learn as much from a mediocre lunch
As from an excellent lunch.
Out the window is a woman
Unable to remove a child's toy from a dog's mouth.
Then a man walks in and confuses you with George.
"George?" he says. "Sorry, I thought you were George," he says.
"I am George," you say, hoping to complicate matters.

III.

## Some Number of Wrongs

Human history has been largely a matter
Of moving from one place to another.
The sad little man emerging from the public washroom.
Lighting a cigarette, sitting down, crossing his legs.
The poor young girl obligated to watch her skateboarding boyfriend.
Prehistoric man probably had strategies for overcoming the hiccups.
Some number of wrongs will eventually make a right.
We just need to be patient and calm and wait here long enough.
The racecar drivers' names will always sound like racecar drivers' names.
The circular reasoning of the racecar driver who drives around in a circle.
It's time for a new kind of failure,
A more gratifying, a more legitimate kind of failure.
The sad little man, sitting down, spilling coffee on himself.

Common Sense


How about we coagulate the sap
From these tropical plants
And see where that gets us!
With any luck we'll
Have vulcanized belts before spring!

Abstract Bicycle
*for Nathan Zimmerman*


In the spring he resolved to take up cycling.
He set out to acquire a bicycle.
He spent considerable energy researching brands and models.
He settled on a model that was to his liking.
He then searched for a retailer
Who could deliver the product at the best possible price.
He looked all around.
Nationwide inquiries were made.
Telephone numbers were called.
Ultimately the model he wanted
Was not available under acceptable conditions.
Alternative models were taken into consideration.
Not the best models, but perfectly good models.
Eventually, a satisfactory model was located at a good price.
But an effort was then made to find it at a *better* price.
He looked and looked some more until
A very good model was found
At probably the best available price.
At this point he was ready to take delivery of the bicycle.
But now it was winter, and his enthusiasm for cycling had passed.
He would wait around another six months
And then he would start the whole process over again.
He would go through this every year.

Fake Snow

The man's suit had enclosures and compartments
And openings and façades and moving parts and hidden seams.
Was the man's suit dishonest or was the man dishonest?
He said that his mission was three-fold.
Fantastic, we thought—here's a man whose mission has *folds* in it.
We wanted to disregard his foldy mission
But he had us cornered in a small room.
He argued that fake snow could be superior to authentic snow.
That was part of his mission, somehow, I remember.
Fake snow, he said, could be periwinkle blue if it wanted to be.
Never tell a fake he can't do something.

Cannellini Beans


It's true that she handed me an adjustable wrench,
But she could have handed it to me *nicer*.
She went to four different stores to find cannellini beans
And she doesn't even *like* cannellini beans.
She said that if we paint this room a dark color
We will make the room look smaller.
Yet, why are we afraid to sense the truth about this room's size?

Macaroni


He was only pretending to see what he wanted to see,
When in reality he was seeing what he actually saw.
The pair of pants that looked like a dead animal on the hallway floor.
The man who appreciates the silver afternoon never gets any credit.
The baby carrots are not really baby carrots—one must use his imagination.
The poem that went somewhere for a while and then stopped going somewhere.
We pretended to be old men for years until we actually were old men.
We bought each other's books largely out of pity.
The ongoing drama of one's fingernails.
The debilitating strokes for different folks.
Must we continue to shape macaroni in new ways?

Tom Will Not Remind You of John

We are what we forgot we were.
We can't even remember
What the one bad apple spoiled for the rest of us.
We trust our memories because we have no choice.
There was once a beautiful idea, but we don't remember what it was.
All we can do is wait for something else to remind us of it.
John will remind you of Tom but Tom will not remind you of John.
One thought will lead to another thought.
Sometimes a thought will refuse to lead to another thought.
Ignorance is a kind of salvation, so if you're not ignorant
You pretend to be ignorant.
Nobody can prove that you're not ignorant.

China Readies Itself for Snow with Tough Talk


I saw this newspaper headline once that read,
*China Readies Itself for Snow with Tough Talk.*
The article, it turned out, wasn't really about snow.
At least not snow in the sense of
Snow falling from the sky or anything like that.
No, it turned out the article was referring to
Treasury Secretary John Snow.
Apparently, Treasury Secretary Snow was going to China.
And the Chinese, apparently,
Were readying themselves for Treasury Secretary Snow.
And the way in which they readied themselves for Snow,
Apparently, was with tough talk.

True Story


We were in a rowboat
On a still lake at dusk
When a fisherman
Wearing an adjustable hat
Shouted across the water
That Princess Diana was dead.

## The Mother of the Poet

The mother of the poet is probably tired
Of explaining to people that her son is a poet.
Her son probably should have made more of an effort
To be involved in something that was simple to brag about.
The mother of the heating contractor does not
Have the same problem as the mother of the poet.
When the mother of the heating contractor talks about her son
It's usually understood, from the beginning, that her son,
The heating contractor, is not pretending to be a heating contractor.
When the mother of the poet talks, the listener will
Begin with the assumption that her son is pretending to be a poet.
The mother of the poet spends a good deal of energy *justifying* her son.
The poet, of course, did not mean
To put his mother in this difficult position.
Or did he?

The Comet


His father died and he inherited his father's car,
Which only reminded him more that his father had died.
But the car itself wouldn't die, refused to die,
Even though he wanted it to die.
It ran so much better than all of the cars
That didn't remind him that his father had died.
It had unattractive plastic seat covers
That protected the seats from becoming unattractive.
But the car would not die, refused to die.
So he decided to have the car repainted.
He sought out the most inexpensive automotive paint shop,
Which is what his father would have done.
He was unaware, though,
That the sample color swatches,
Posted on the wall of the shop,
Were terribly faded from the sun.
So the car he never chose,
From the father he never chose,
Was now a color he never chose.
He held on to the car for a reasonable period of time,
An honorable period of time,
Until he could justify selling it.

Experiment

When my brother was a kid
He conducted an experiment with a guinea pig.
He wanted to see how long a guinea pig could go
Without food and water.
"Four days!" he said proudly at the end of his study.

Duck Decoys


There was a man once who tried
In all seriousness to woo my mother
By making duck decoys for her—
Making duck decoys with his bare hands,
Sending them to our house in the mail.
He wanted to impress my mother with duck decoys,
Duck decoys that he built all by himself.
That's what this man was trying to do.
He was trying to lure a woman
With something designed to lure a duck.

The Horizon

He could take perfectly sensible ideas
And he could explain them until they made no sense.
Either that or he was bad at explaining things.
Confusing explanations could be developed into an art form.
Misinformation and the wrong words—
Those seem like the best places to start.
If we all took a little more time,
We could help each other not understand things a little better.
Anything to make it harder to get through the day.
The horizon is a conspiracy of sorts.
Not understanding a low-pressure system can bring comfort.
Suddenly you bear no responsibility for the low-pressure system.
You bear no responsibility for sub atomic particles.
The answer is less interesting than the possible answer.
The possible answer has the allure of possibility.
He didn't win our respect until he confused us.
I knew him back before he was confusing
And he was not impressive at all.
Then he started confusing everyone,
He confused everyone into taking him seriously.

## Not Everything is Funny

My contribution to mankind has been small, but I've seen smaller.
The man who wanted to borrow my friend's wife's urine for a drug test.
You never know when your friend's wife's urine will be in demand.
Poetry is something that is captured, like a wild bird.
What good is that memory of buying an umbrella in Boston?
The bowling alley is open and the windows of the bowling alley are open.
For every two people in this town
There's one person who looks like two people.
The dandelions in this town are taken more seriously than I am.
Everything is serious but not everything is funny.

The Way It Used to Sound

We had seen paintings like those before
But we hadn't really seen them for a while.
The last time we saw them, we were very
Hungry and we had to go to the bathroom.
It was a story that had been told before,
But it needed to be told again.
There were other stories that had also been told before
That did not need to be told again.
It was a film that we had seen before
But we weren't really wearing our glasses.
The characters in the novel were wearing
Clothes that seemed more like short story clothes.
The author's description of the character's face sounded
Too much like an author's description of a character's face.
We liked the way it *used* to sound, the way it sounded *before.*
Could you please make it sound that way again?

By Watching


The way that my father cleaned up cat vomit
Was a tremendous influence on the way that I clean up cat vomit.
He had the personal charisma to convince
Another man to buy a swallow-tailed jacket.
He drove across international borders to purchase premium steak sauce.
*His* father drove across state lines to buy ketchup.
You are your parents in wretched excess.
We swatted flies with the alternative newspaper.
The period between the indentured servitude of living with your parents
And the indentured servitude of being a parent.
Abandoning the dearest of friends in exchange for underground parking.
The guilt one suffers when jaywalking in front of a child.
I suppose we learned how to wait in a waiting room
By watching our parents wait in a waiting room.

IV.

The Davenport Flood

She seemed unaware that her arm was around a half-wit.
One should always be aware when one's arm is around a half-wit.
Friends don't let friends have their arms around a half-wit.
A man who had gained regional notoriety
Because he had predicted the Davenport flood.
Her arm was around the man who had predicted the Davenport flood.

Her eyes were as big as paper plates.
Does she even remember the stupid jokes you told her ten years ago?
How she made you feel the way you feel
When you find a five-dollar bill in an old winter coat.
Her eyes actually *were* as big as paper plates.

It was a thrill just to watch her pack up her personal belongings
And walk out the door.

He would eat chicken salad sandwiches
With authorities on Alexander the Great.
He would remove his glasses before he ate lunch.
If his lunch fell out of focus, it was a matter of indifference to him.
He rarely complained about anything, but he was
Very good at complaining, and he should have done it more often.
He was not so much a reactionary, as he was
Someone who preferred the progressives of the past.
His favorite smell, he said, was the inside of an old British car.
When you add cream and butter to poison, he said,
You end up with really rich poison.
He said the rationalizations of the avant-garde
Were akin to poor sportsmanship.
He was mostly hot air, but it was an exquisite, rarefied hot air.
You would meet him for coffee, and he would have
Unexplained bandages on his face.
He enjoyed most what he called,
The Brutal Amusement of Walking Around the Block.

An Aluminum Houseboat in the Sky

They were not so much unidentified flying objects
As they were unexplainable flying machines,
Or airplanes that didn't really look like airplanes,
More along the lines of iridescent prefabricated birds,
Flickering experimental gaslight beer signs,
A kind of sinister paper airplane streaming with Christmas lights,
Only more round and more shiny than a paper airplane—
An aluminum houseboat in the sky that had burned to the ground.

Amtrak

I took the train out west to see my mother.
I found myself in the lounge car talking to a stereo aficionado.
He told me he had a *halfway decent* stereo in his truck.
He talked like that, he said things like *basically* and *halfway decent.*
He understood how sound traveled through a wire.
He understood the workings of remote wireless signals.
He could explain how hotel reservations flew through the sky.
We went past an Alpo dog food factory in Nebraska.
I remember the newspapers were about
Russian submarine men trapped at the bottom of the sea.
Then a weird hardwood floor guy joined our conversation.
He refinished hardwood floors, that was his identity.
At first I thought he was insane, and then I thought he was a Christian,
And then it turned out he was a gluehead.
But he was also a Christian and he was also insane.
He had absorbed polyurethane through his mucous membranes
Throughout his hardwood floor career.
He sat there with his crazy Christian gluehead smile.
But he carried himself well—
He carried himself with dignity and elegance.
He was like the *consummate* gluehead, the *gluehead's* gluehead.

## Factors

The snapping turtle, his arguments having no legal force,
Was reduced to making circular movements with his head.
The book about the conjoined twins was only good up to the point
Where they were wrongly accused of stealing peacock feathers.
It's possible, then as now, to justify one's foolishness
By cloaking it in a kind of ridiculous beauty.
The determined man will come to understand the white sea birds
By plotting factors along a horizontal axis.
(It's funny until somebody becomes a Christian.)
The sustained groaning of copulating tortoises on public television.
The determined man will finally determine
That the white birds are self-involved and conceited.
The time has come to plot metaphors along a horizontal axis.

When the Drunk Man Speaks Loudly

When the drunk man speaks loudly,
It's easier for us to hear what he's saying.
When the drunk man repeats a phrase,
It tends to reinforce his theme.
When the drunk man grabs your shoulder,
He's looking to create a sense of intimacy.
Sometimes it's possible to find the bathroom by
Going downstairs and using common sense.
When two men argue about whether or not
They have flying cockroaches in New Orleans,
It's best just to keep quiet and try to learn something.
I walk by this bar every day and there's always
Laundry vapor billowing out of a basement vent.
What the hell are they laundering down there—
*Bar towels?*

Your Obsolete Passion

Your obsolete passion is the most interesting thing about you.
Your tragic delusions are what make you so adorable.
You're an unnecessary genius taking up perfectly good space.
You say that America has the best strangers in its parking lots—
That we should always judge a culture
By the way it treats its strangers in its parking lots.
You took bad poems that were never any good,
And you sat down and made them worse.
In your spiral notebook, you took out
Your rage at incompetent handymen.
You taught us to take better care of our bad ideas.
You taught us not to be so wasteful with our bad ideas.
You told the young poets not to revise their poetry.
You wanted the young poets to follow your example.
You wanted to weaken the competition.

It Might Bring Happiness

The promise of the empty sheet of paper.
You can't decide whether the rain is making you nervous or not.
The tingling sensation in your leg will go unexplained.
Circumstances require that it go unexplained.
The tingling sensation in your leg isn't the only
Thing that needs explaining around here.

In his dream the secret police were questioning him
But then he woke up and they were gone.
They would have you killed if you wore wire-rimmed spectacles.
If your vision had deteriorated, it suggested enlightenment.
What happened to the promise of the empty sheet of paper?
The oldest excuse in the book should command more respect, he thought.

He enjoyed the company of incoherent men.
But all of his favorite incoherent men had moved away.
It was not clear whether the incoherent men enjoyed his company.
But that was to be expected; making things clear wasn't their strong suit.

It's Possible

It's possible that death is a lot of fun.
Death might be very similar to a bowl of ice cream.
We shouldn't judge eternity until all the facts are in.

The eyes of the dead fish are far from encouraging.
But we shouldn't get all worked up about that.
I was enjoying myself until I noticed that I was enjoying myself.

Sometimes you get tired of *noticing* things.
Inspiration will come on like a bad headache.
Some erections will make it difficult to walk through double doors.

The broken man with the handful of candy and the hardcover book,
Emptying his ketchup and his mustard into his ashtray,
Hearing a joke that his dead friend would have liked.

The Ghost of Your Mom

We never imagine that a ghost might be disappointed with herself.
The ghost of your mom is probably more unhappy now than ever.
The ghost of your mom is probably still beating herself up over
The same things she was always beating herself up over.
The ghost of your mom is probably wishing
She had accomplished more as a ghost,
Setting impossible ghost standards for herself.
The ghost of your mom is probably wondering
What she's going to do when she gets off of work.
We tend to think only of *the advantages*
Of being the ghost of your mom.

The Unapproachable Butcher


The unapproachable butcher and the unflappable baker
And the unassailable candlestick maker with his sad sack story
About market forces bearing down on candlestick makers and
The fireman with his unknowable suspenders and
The chicken crossing the road, the unspeakable road, and
The blinking light of the faraway radio tower, and
The menthol cigarette smoker with the tiny
Fiberglass trees growing in his lungs,
And the square peg, the uninspired square peg,
And the uninspired round hole, and all like that,
And the army traveling on its stomach, its theoretical stomach,
The stomach that hasn't had an army traveling on it for quite some time.

He Thought He Saw a Bug

He thought he saw a bug crawling in his food,
But he wasn't really sure what he saw.
Either there was a bug crawling in his food,
Or he was imagining that bugs were crawling in his food.
He couldn't decide which was worse.
He would prefer not to be hallucinating bugs.
On the other hand, if he had to eat a bug,
He would prefer it was an imaginary bug.

And it wasn't even a very *impressive* bug either,
Which only made him feel more pathetic.
I mean there he was, sitting all alone,
Wondering if he was imagining unimpressive bugs.

God Poem


God's been kind of set in his ways lately.
God's been playing his cards close to his chest.
God's got a lot on his plate these days.
God's up to his earballs in a lot of routine paperwork.
God's one of those guys who can walk and chew gum at the same time.
But when God threw the baby out with the bathwater
That really boiled everybody's potatoes.
God didn't get where he is by kissing a lot of ass.

The Strong Silent Man


Those who wish to be judged
By their deeds not their words
Never have anything interesting to say.
The strong silent man always fills me with dread.
Let me be remembered as the weak noisy man.
The weak silent man can also be dreadful,
But at least he's weak—at least he's got that going for him.
The strong noisy man can be of some interest,
But he typically has a restraining order against him.
Give me the weak clamorous man! The strong crybaby!
The loudmouth hypochondriac! The uproarious pantywaist!
Mamas don't let your babies grow up to be strong silent men!
Let them be bombastic cowards in love with the sound of their own voice.
The strong silent man will not inherit the Earth.
The strong silent man is bad company.
Who will publish the oral history of the strong silent man?
Let me throw spiritual sand in the eyes of the strong silent man.
Let me be the gushy advocate for the superficial weakling,
With all of his feeble, empty talk.

Handshakes


It appears that people are
No longer contriving unusual handshakes.
It's looking more like people are satisfied
With the handshakes already available to them.
The prevailing handshakes of the moment.
The half-poet is satisfied with lightweight surrealism.
It's a celebration of inconsequential disorder,
Which is the best kind of disorder.
The identical blonde women with the simultaneous sneezing fits.
The vending machine will cloud one's
Reasoning with a kind of low-grade passion.
The vending machine will offer nonsense
That appears to make sense momentarily.
In other words, it's a miracle.

Those Days are Gone Now


Americans once wrote good songs about boll weevils.
Outstanding poetic laments were composed about snout beetles.
America was producing fantastic songs about vermin at one time.
But not anymore—those days are gone now.
There hasn't been a good song about vermin for years.


We had squirrels in our attic, so we called up the squirrel people.
They sent a man right over to deal with the squirrels.
The thing was, the man they sent over *looked* exactly like a squirrel.
I mean ridiculously like a squirrel.
My friend McNally used to bring his cat to this veterinarian,
And the veterinarian looked exactly like a cat.
I mean freakishly like a cat.
Face completely covered in cat features.


The best book you can read
About controlling squirrels
Is called *Outwitting Squirrels*.
I haven't read the book myself,
I'm just paraphrasing what the squirrel guy told me.
You wait until it's dark out,
And then you put a bright light in the attic.
Then you walk around the perimeter of the house.
And you can see the light coming through
The squirrel openings in the roof.
Before you seal those openings
You drive the squirrels away with talk radio.

Small transistor radios placed in the eaves.
The radios talking all the time.
The disturbing human voice coming through.
The tiny squirrel eardrums having about all they can stand.

Funny Grimaces


The poets are working hard at saying things about the moon.
The poets are generally unconcerned with
Whether or not you're having any fun.
Not enough poets are talking about
How the electricity is different in Europe.
It remains unclear why people make
Funny grimaces when they squeeze a lemon.
Writers will write about writing more than bakers will bake about baking.
The sophomoric observations will turn out to have been right all along.
Subtlety is fine but it needs to be used sparingly.
Sometimes nothing will do
But to dislodge food from somebody's windpipe.
The elephants will come in through the service entrance.
I apologize for any inconvenience my poetry has caused.